*To Marie,
Great to work with you.*

SHEEP. SHEPHERD. DOG.

BUILDING A MAGNIFICENT TEAM AROUND YOU

*Enjoy the read.
Chris*

CHRIS FARNSWORTH

© 2015 CHRIS FARNSWORTH

ALL RIGHTS RESERVED. NO PART OF THIS WORK MAY BE REPRODUCED OR STORED IN AN INFORMATIONAL RETRIEVAL SYSTEM, WITHOUT THE EXPRESS PERMISSION OF THE PUBLISHER IN WRITING.

ISBN:97815174910000

PUBLISHED BY:

Contents

Foreword	i
Acknowledgments	v
Introduction	1
Chapter 1: Are you the sheep, shepherd or dog?	3
Chapter 2: So what is it about sheep?	11
Chapter 3: What makes a good shepherd?	23
Chapter 4: A dog is a man's best friend — or is it?	35
Chapter 5: K.I.S.S. — Keep It Simple, Shepherd (for the sheep)	45
Chapter 6: Assessing the right dog for the team	59
Chapter 7: How would ewe react to the dog?	69
Chapter 8: Building that magnificent team	77
An offer from Chris Farnsworth	89
About the author	93

*To my brilliant partner
for all her help and ongoing support.*

Foreword

*"There are no rules here –
we're trying to accomplish something"*
Thomas Edison

"Hi, nice to meet you, thanks for coming, what do you do?"

"I'm a shepherd and I have an idea for a book; it's called 'Are you the sheep, shepherd or dog in your life'?"

I was a bit dismissive if I'm honest. It had been a long day, I'd just done a two-hour presentation in front of 2000 people, I still had a bit of jet-lag and I'd shaken hands with a lot of people.

A few minutes later I thought "Hang on a minute, a shepherd? What's a shepherd doing at an entrepreneurs conference? And what was that book idea again? Sheep shepherd dog? Wow, that actually is a bit different."

Fast forward a few months and I can guarantee that Chris is indeed 'a bit different' – and this is his strength.

Yes, he really is a shepherd. But not your 'normal' shepherd (no offence to any shepherds reading this!). Chris is a challenger who throws out the rulebook and always sees things from a different perspective. Not just his viewpoint either; the key to being a good shepherd in his opinion, as you will discover in this book, is the ability – and willingness – to see things from others' perspectives. As a contract shepherd Chris has years of experience in attracting customers, negotiating with them, earning their respect and juggling an immense workload, which at one time meant his caring for 6500 sheep with his loyal colleagues – two Border Collie sheepdogs.

Typical of Chris' curiosity and ability to ask good questions, a chance meeting with a business associate of his partner Caroline led him to conjure up the concept of team building with the aid of sheep. Several voluntary sessions with groups of teenagers helped him develop the blueprint, and Raising the Baa was born, as a result of companies asking him to come and work with their teams.

His company works with clients such as Airbus, Mondelez International (formerly Kraft Foods), Volkswagen, Clarks

Sheep. Shepherd. Dog.

and IKEA, to name just a few, all practically applying the principles of that formidable team 'One Man and his Dog' (as the BBC TV series refers to it) to their own businesses.

I'm delighted to have played my part to encourage and assist Chris in getting this book to market as quickly as possible. You will learn loads, I know, and my hope is that you, like Chris, will challenge the status quo, view situations with a different perspective from now on – and of course build the most awesome team around you.

Raymond Aaron
NY Times Bestselling Author

Acknowledgements

Writing this book has made me realise just how many people (and animals!) have shaped my life through their teachings, friendship, mentoring, love and support – and often a mix of all.

I appreciate that there is a distinct risk of my missing someone by mentioning people by name, so in advance I apologise if my ageing memory has got the better of me at the time of going to print!

So here goes... In no particular order other than how people have sprung to mind, I would like to thank:

My family and friends
Dad (RIP), thanks for being inspired by BBC's The Good Life and adopting the self-sufficient lifestyle during my teenage years, bringing me my first experience of handling livestock. And Mum for putting up with our efforts and wanting everything 'oven-ready'! Thanks to you both for your never-ending belief in me and for all your love and support naturally.

My son Giles for all your help over the years with the sheep, despite it being your least favourite job, and for your frequent reminders that I'm a sad old shepherd who works far too hard!

Caroline, my long-suffering partner in both the home and at work, thanks for badgering me to get this book out there and for all your help with it. Sorry for being such a grumpy old s-d at times!

Probably my longest-standing shepherding friend, Robin – thanks for our extraordinary working relationship, the amazing times we've spent around sheep and at parties (not at the same time) and for being a part of my life for so long.

One of my newest friends and fellow villager, Greg, for the laughs over those sneaky beers and especially for elevating my sofa so I could comfortably get this book written whilst recuperating from my hip surgery.

Business connections
To all my shepherding contract customers for the experiences and challenges that your flocks have provided me; I am indebted for your business.

Sheep. Shepherd. Dog.

To those in charge of networking and other business groups who have given me the opportunity to share my story and words of shepherding wisdom. A particular shout-out has to go to Steve Dye who entitled my upcoming talk 'Are you the Sheep, Shepherd or Dog in your business?' and to all those who encouraged me to write a book on the subject.

When Foot & Mouth temporarily devastated my sheep business I had to secure another source of income and I am eternally grateful for my introduction by Jean Hyatt to direct selling company Forever Living Products. I simply couldn't function without the aloe products (and they have helped my animals on many occasions), and the company introduced me to the whole world of personal development. The two UK country managers, Dusty Greene (RIP) and Bob Parker, have always inspired me with their uncomplicated, upfront and calm leadership, and Dusty specifically brought a new word into my vocabulary: 'sticktoitiveness' – a must for everyone in business.

My insatiable desire for personal improvement led me to invest in training events, and I would particularly like to thank Christopher Howard and his team of trainers for the huge amount of knowledge imparted. Clare Smale of

Inspired2Learn, thank you for helping me broaden my experience of the world of NLP and introduce it to my world of shepherding.

Another thank you to my partner Caroline, this time for letting me gate-crash her meeting with a certain David Wreathall, who at the time was just launching his youth development charity Inner Flame. The original agenda of the meeting got somewhat sidelined and the outcome, some years later, turned into an accidental business. Thank you David for letting me evolve the concept with the numerous groups of wonderful youngsters on your courses – the best marketing research you could ever wish for!

To Warren Cass of Business Scene, I'm so grateful for the opportunity to trial 'team building with sheep' with adults, from which the hitherto voluntary concept swiftly transferred into a full-time enterprise.

Massive thanks to Martin Warnes for naming and branding the business Raising the Baa, and for all your ongoing support and brand guardianship. To Ian 'Vino' for pulling together our first website to meet a national media deadline, I thank you. And we would not have developed as fast in our first year without the mentoring and guidance from the guys at Business Copilot – your input remains very much appreciated.

To the teams from too many companies to mention, thank you for taking on the challenge of herding sheep and for spreading the word to all your colleagues and friends. To all the farmers and our fabulous conference centre partners, it is a pleasure to work with you all, and we look forward to an ever more fruitful association.

Accounting and book-keeping are two skills that I most definitely lack, and I am forever grateful to my long-standing (and suffering) team Jill and Jeremy – you are both amazing and have saved me £££ over the decades I'm sure!

The book
My support team has most recently expanded to include all those who have helped with the creation of this, my first book. So to Raymond Aaron for your awesome book-writing course, to Anita Shead the so aptly named speedy typist for putting my ramblings onto paper, to Roy Freeman for designing the cover, to Noel Ford for the chapter cartoons and to Caroline (again!) for all the editing, spelling and grammar checking (far better than Google!) and for writing the bits that I found a challenge.

My biggest inspiration of all
The thousands of sheep I've worked with over the last few decades and my faithful and gorgeous dogs Mist, Frost, Drizzle, Effie and Gale – the best colleagues anyone could ask for.

Chris Farnsworth
Wiltshire
January 2015

Introduction

At first glance this book may appear to be only about sheep, dogs and stories from the shepherding world.

Having been a shepherd for over 30 years I naturally do have many stories to share. But it's the lessons that are gleaned from these experiences that form the backbone of this book.

The aim of this book is to help you, the reader, understand how people react with each other and see things from others' points of view. Leadership of a team can be challenging and often it might be because we receive little training in this area. What motivates the team and how the members tick can be hard to fathom. Emotional attachment and office politics can cloud your vision of the way ahead for the team.

We sometimes look at a situation and see only one solution.

Sheep and dogs are more like us than you might imagine. Understanding the mindset of these animals helps us see situations in a fresh light and can help us reach a different conclusion. An alternative outlook and working well together helps the team achieve so much more.

I guess I've taken for granted the way in which I've always managed and communicated with my teams of dogs and sheep. Consequently it's been fascinating for me to transfer my knowledge and shepherding skills into the business world for the last few years. I continue to be inspired by clients who bring their teams to experience training programmes of my company, Raising the Baa. It seems to me that whether people work in aviation, engineering, food manufacturing, retailing, charity or a football club, the lessons are all the same.

So I wonder which character's traits will seem most similar to your's? Sheep, shepherd or dog?

Chapter 1

Are you the sheep, shepherd or dog?

When faced with this question, and I've asked it hundreds of times over the last few years, it's amazing the variety of responses people give.

Some people don't want to answer the question; they feel possibly that it is a bit intrusive; it will tell me something about them that they would not want me to know. Asking this question out of the blue can be very revealing about how they deal with unexpected situations. On the other hand, most people find it an intriguing question, something they've never thought about before.

Most people will try to pick one of the three characters to fit their whole life. Most will think of the sheep at first glance, as the one that is lowest down the pecking order. It's the animal that appears to be stupid and simple, and simply follows the others. Yet they have the impression of being light and fluffy, warm and cuddly, just being out there in the field simply grazing. A very simple life with very little to worry about. That sums up the sheep. So most people will dismiss the sheep: it's not like them, as life could not be that simple, or they wouldn't want it to be like that.

Their mind then turns to the shepherd. In their mind the shepherd is the one that makes all the decisions, is in control and is perceived to be at the top of the pecking order. This is more like it, at the top where they have control of what happens in their life. They are the ones making the decisions, setting the tasks and agendas for each day, the ones who look after everything. The shepherd is in their eyes the boss who sets the pace and direction for everybody else.

Thoughts then turn to the dog. They feel the dog is intelligent as well, but it is the one running around the sheep and doing all the work.. They get the sheep in the pen and the shepherd is there simply to close the gate.

Often people will relate to this feeling; they are the ones doing all the work and somebody else just comes along and closes the gate to finish it off. Then the "shepherd" gets all the praise and glory, for doing a good job, appearing to care so much, although the dog has actually done 90% of the work to allow for the sheep to end up in the pen. All the dog gets is a small pat on the back, if it is lucky. A Bonio or some food at the end of the day and that is it, yet nothing would have happened without their work.

The look of horror on people's faces when they think that they might be the dog!

Oh my gosh, that is just like my life. Not just my job. Therefore I must be the dog. Oh gosh. That is the wrong answer isn't it? That's not right, I must do something about this. Why have I not noticed this until now?

This is a common response to the sheep shepherd or dog question. People often think that the shepherd is the "right" answer and any other is not being the best they can be.

For me, there is no right or wrong answer; there is simply a state of mind. The mindset of the sheep, the shepherd and the dog is very different.

http://bit.do/RUSSD

The sheep's mindset is predominantly one of little ambition. If food and water are available, the sheep really does not try to better itself at all. It will take and accept whatever life gives it.

The dog, on the other hand, is a lot more ambitious; it wants to do the best it can. Being top of the pack, the best it can be, having some control of what is around it, and having some effect on those around it. This is really important to the dog and it will work really hard to achieve that status. It also knows that working together as "the pack" will achieve so much more. The dogs are real team players and they know that they can be a powerful group. Any more than one dog can become a hunting pack with egos and personalities. Competition between dogs can be helpful at times, but can easily get out of control.

So what is the mindset of a good shepherd? Do they see themselves at the top of the tree? They obviously have responsibility for the animals under their care, the sheep as well as the dogs. Both animals are very different so need to be handled accordingly. The shepherd also has to manage his own mindset. The shepherd needs to make judgements every single day; what's best to do on a day-to-day basis. Not only are they working with the animals,

Sheep. Shepherd. Dog.

but also with Mother Nature, which can sometimes be a phenomenal force to fight against.

For the shepherd, the care of the sheep is really important. This is equally as important as having his faithful friend with him, his dog which is his right hand man. The shepherd has to set achievable tasks, not too high, as well as making life as easy as possible, for the dog, the sheep, as well as for himself. Shepherds often can't work effectively in the rain (thank you Mother Nature). They will take a look at the sheep but they know that when it is raining it is a lot harder to work with the animals. The dogs are not quite so keen, the sheep are very wet and slippery to handle and if it is really heavy rain they will look for shelter themselves. I would say it is not a "win-win" situation.

When it is a hot sunny day shepherds will start early to make use of the cooler weather in the morning, or work late into the balmy evening. This is a "win-win" because the sheep are cooler, they'll be rested; and the dogs will work better because they do not get so hot. Finally for the shepherd, getting the work done in the early morning when it is cooler means they can relax in the afternoon and evening, or if things have not gone so well finish off in the evening. When all three parties are in harmony life is wonderful. Getting that "win, win, win" situation is so important, not only in shepherding but in life in general.

Chapter 2

So what is it about sheep?

Most people will see sheep as stupid, as they will blindly follow the rest and will not have any independent thoughts from the rest of the flock. As a shepherd I see sheep in a very different light – the sheep lives its life very much in the comfort zone. There's nothing wrong with being in the comfort zone, and most of us will want to stay there some of the time. From that zone we will form habits that can serve us well. We don't need to think too much about what we do, and we form some great routines.

Take sleeping – our body likes to get up more or less at the same time every day, we'll go to a job we know, sit in the same place, travel the same way to and from the job, because we know and like the routine. At the end of the day we'll go back to bed more or less at the same time. The sheep very much follow that same pattern. They want an easy life and they hate change. When you put sheep into a new field, the first thing they do is walk around the perimeter of the field, checking out their environment, just visually checking so they have some reference of where they are.

They'll check out all the fencing or the natural barriers that might trap them in a tricky situation. They'll look for the gaps that they might venture through in the future, but it's a visual thing at first. We also take a lot from first impression, making judgement about people and places. The sheep are just making themselves aware of the environment and where they can run if necessary. Later the sheep will physically test the fence, whether they can slip through a gap, whether they can smell or see something appealing on the other side.

A sheep will push hard at the physical barrier of the fence, so much so that it will get stuck trying to get to what it wants. So what happens when you put sheep on a hillside where there are no barriers; just that wide open space? The sheep have the right to roam over the whole mountainside, but they stay in one particular area and make up their own boundaries. They will create a river or the top of a mountain as a boundary, and they will stay in this area where they feel comfortable, and will only move out of that area once the food has run out or when they are gathered by shepherds.

The amazing thing is that when the sheep return to the mountain they will seek out the same area to live in again. The advantage of knowing an area like this is that they know where everything is and are familiar with the other sheep sharing the same space. So if the lambs are born into the area, the knowledge of this part of the mountain will be handed down through generations. They also will be brought up knowing the other sheep around them. They would know how others react to danger and where to run to get away from any bad weather. So the sheep become totally familiar not only with their environment but also the behaviours of the other sheep around them.

Just as we can have characters around us with whom we feel comfortable, we belong to a group, and this makes us feel safe in that area. This might relate to a street, village or even a town where we live. We can have large family groups living together, not only in the sheep world but also in our world. We have a word for the sheep that migrate to a particular area, and that is called hefting. This is great for the shepherd because it means you don't need to put up fencing and yet you will know where your sheep will be. A win on both sides.

Shepherds will still give the sheep a visual mark to make clear the ownership of them. This is done at the time of the first gathers when the lambs still stay close to their mother. When the sheep are released they will work their own way back to stay in their comfortable zone on the mountain.

I think this is very interesting; how many times when we try and change a habit do we end up back doing the same thing a few weeks later? I think it is highlighted when people win large sums of money, and often they're in the same financial situation as before the win five years later.

They've gone back to that comfortable zone where their beliefs and their values lie.

So even though they've been given a lot of money they'll end up at the same level of investments and knowledge.

The sheep are going back to what they know, going back to that comfortable area, hefting to that particular hillside. Can shepherds change that behaviour? With time, physical barriers and hard work you can change the sheep's comfortable area. At lambing time this becomes more important. The ewe will sniff the area really carefully and it will have got to know the smell of its lamb via her waters. Now the interesting thing is that when the lamb comes out it stays in the area; it will connect to its mother in that area and will define the comfortable zone to run to. If you leave lambs alone they will still be there two or three days after they have been born, still locked into that area. The lambs know the smell, and will know the sheep around them so they will be able to easily recognise their mother. Of course it works both ways as the mother knows where that smell is strongest and will find her baby quickly. The interesting thing is that if we move them off they will lose that connection unless it is firmly embedded in their brain, making visual and audio links as well. Until this happens, it's quite imperative that they stay in that area where they are both comfortable. Where they know what's going on. Often the ewe, if the flock is stressed, will run back to that area and expect to find its lamb there. Likewise when we are ill or stressed it's natural for us to want to stay comfortable and run back home for that TLC. Feeling safe and in good hands is not only when we are ill; it can happen when we are passengers, when we want to have confidence in the driver or pilot to overcome any sense of fear.

When the sheep have a physical barrier how does it impact their lives? Containing sheep behind netting, gates and other barriers through which they can't physically push is great for the shepherd to know where the sheep are, but it can be expensive. We've developed electric fencing where it's a psychological barrier; 7,000 volts goes round the wire and gives them a small electric charge that gives them a tap on the nose to stop them from going any further.

Not understanding where this "tap" has come from, the sheep run back into their comfortable zone.

They stay where they are comfortable and yet they can clearly see through the electric fence knowing that there's plenty of grass on the other side.

We can use this electric fencing to subdivide a field, to keep different flocks separate. This is a psychological barrier that they can run through but the thought of the electric fencing stops them, even though it is only a momentary bit of discomfort. They see the grass and they'd love to have more of it. It looks enticing and yet this little wire gives them that little tap on the nose, and they don't understand where it comes from or how it works, so the sheep are held by their own mind. You can keep several hundred sheep behind three strands of electric wire, yet none of them will go over it. If they see sheep the other side they will simply call to them, most probably saying something along the lines of "How did you get over there?" or "It looks great over there." Nevertheless that psychological barrier will stop them going towards what they want. How many times in life are we stopped by those seemingly mental barriers that we have, created by those limiting beliefs that we hold on to?

Sheep are not great at challenging those limiting beliefs. Even if the fence isn't switched on, or it has been taken away, there will be one or two sheep that will go across the line on the ground, challenge it, feel that nothing happens and discover that they can venture off. Slipping beneath it or potentially jumping it takes a lot more courage but once it has been learnt, they will get to the greener grass on the other side. There will always be some sheep braver than others, and even though the majority of the flock are the other side of the fence the rest will not go across it. Just like some people with fear; no matter what others are saying around them, they will not take the next step. We all need to challenge the psychological barrier to see how far we can go towards a goal.

Now the interesting thing is, when the sheep see danger coming, whichever is the smaller number will move to the others, to the safety of the flock. The sheep will run back though the electric fence, with great gusto. Why? The drive to get back to safety is far greater than the desire for more food. Once the sheep know they can go through the electric fence they will continue to do it as long as it is beneficial to them. So once their internal barrier has been broken down the fence becomes no more than a slight irritant to what they want.

http://bit.do/SoWhatSheep

Does this sound similar to your life? Are you the one who pushes your own boundaries, prepared to be the odd one out standing on the other side of the 'electric fence'? Or are you the one who, once you are shown, will follow the first sheep or stay in the flock no matter what?

So we've observed how sheep love to be in the comfort zone and that there's nothing wrong with being comfortable. It allows us at times to daydream and that's really important for creativity, to have wild thoughts, imagination, have those really great ideas that come about when we have that freedom to be comfortable. Sheep have really cracked living in the "now" moment. They're not at all worried about what might happen.

Sheep. Shepherd. Dog.

In fact I had one occasion, which I don't often relate, where I was unloading sheep in the middle of the night. I'd run out of time, it was dark, this was the last load of the day and I really wanted to get this whole flock moved and put all the sheep in the trailer. I guess I was a little bit tired so when I felt all the sheep were unloaded I closed the tailgate and went home.

A couple of days later, even though I had walked past the trailer twice every day, I heard a sheep bleating. I thought that's really funny, I didn't see any sheep around me, the only possibility ... oh my gosh, there is a sheep left in the trailer, how long has it been there? It's been there a couple of days, no food, no water, I felt awful, I felt really gutted.

I thought the first thing I had to do was let it out to eat some grass at the minimum, offer it a bucket of water, just so that it could get some energy back in it. I'm lucky to have even noticed this sheep. I noticed because it made a noise. It was quite happy in the trailer; it must have seen and heard me approach, but it stood dead still I didn't notice it time and time again. Over two days! Eventually it decided the only thing it could do was bleat.

Once I was aware that it was there, I let it out and let it have some grass. Now the interesting part for me is, how long would it take for the sheep to feel full enough to now look for some mates as there was none around? I thought it would be okay there for some time ... well it had food. Actually this sheep had a few mouthfuls of food, had a little bit to drink, literally the smallest mouthful of water, and then was off looking around for its mates. Within two minutes it was happy to move on... it had immediately satisfied its most important need, a few mouthfuls of grass, and it was now looking for company. This was very interesting. Why? Because if that was a human left in a bus or a plane or locked up for a few days, what is the thing they would do the most? They would probably complain bitterly during their captivity and for a long time afterwards to anybody who would listen. Yet the sheep was wanting only to move on and find its mates, to be part of the community and get to know its surroundings. This to me is a fantastic lesson on getting over ourselves.

The sheep are so good at living in the "now" moment.

It doesn't matter what happened in the past, we're okay now, so let's just enjoy it.

Chapter 3

What makes a good shepherd?

The first thing the shepherd needs to be able to do is to deal with the detail. We look after the sheep and treat them one sheep at a time. We lamb one sheep at a time, we shear one sheep at a time, we foot-trim one sheep at a time. Everything is about the detail; how well we observe the sheep's behaviour is really important, and reacting to them in the right way. Often the observations of the little things do matter; the little gestures around your team members do matter. Noticing how somebody looks, what time they turn up and even in the middle of lambing it is important to say "Good morning" as this will set the energy for the day.

The other thing the shepherd needs to do is have a long-term plan, a vision of what will happen for the next day, week, month or year. Even ten years down the line you still need to know what's going to happen, but more importantly what you want to achieve. Breeding programmes can take as long as 100, or even 200 years before you can see some real improvement. The key is not only to have a vision for yourself but to be able to pass it on for others to continue. The greater the clarity, the easier it is to inspire others and create a vision so that others will help you get there. Just making sheep better and/or larger is not focused enough. All the detail needs to be clear so people understand what is wanted and, more importantly, why.

These two factors alone do not make a good shepherd. In fact they just make a very ordinary shepherd. Why? It is not just having the short-term and the long-term vision, although this would give me a job as a shepherd. The animals demand more, and so do people. The third of the three things which I feel make a good shepherd is

being able to see situations from not only your own point of view but also the sheep's and the dog's perspectives.

Not coming from a farming family, I remember asking lots of questions about why the sheep were behaving in a particular way, why the dog was reacting to its environment and why we didn't try some new things now and again. Like many people, farmers don't like a lot of change. Keeping things the same is the comfortable thing to do, although Mother Nature is of course a challenge since it's out of our control. Routine tasks can become more arduous when taking into account the unpredictable nature of the weather.

Big changes can be scary but can yield great returns as well. Going along with what everybody else is doing will give the same results as everybody else. Doing something new, bold and adventurous, however, even with the fear of it all going wrong, can give massive results. We can exert some control of the weather conditions by, for example, working in a barn rather than outdoors so that it is more comfortable for humans. The potential disadvantage is the animals could develop more diseases or other health and welfare issues.

I remember when I worked on a sheep dairy unit and getting the milk out of the udder was the main issue. With cows the teats are at the bottom of the udder after years of breeding. With the sheep they are on the side, not great for a machine. So someone in the sheep world invented a lever which temporarily alters the shape, by lifting the middle part of the udder so that the teats end up at the bottom.

Keeping everything very simple and very effective.

The essential element of this invention was that it made life easier for all parties concerned.

The effort to achieve a result is what we always weigh up. Let's face it; animals make judgement calls all the time. I find if we can make the task easy to do then things get done. Make it difficult and it becomes a battle of wills.

Getting to understand the mindset of people, dogs, even sheep, and appreciate how they view the world is key to getting the best from your team.

The best way of solving issues, conflicts or even coming up with a "win-win" situation is to view the challenge from another's position.

I believe this to be key to being an outstanding shepherd, to building that awesome team around you, to really understanding the characters you work with. It's been said by many that we will replicate the five people with whom we spend the most time, be that in terms of intelligence, financial wealth, behaviours or mindset. The people around you will either hold you back or encourage you, and finding a way that it will work will be about the team you surround yourself with. If you wanted to get the sheep in the pen would you want other shepherds in your team or a bunch of people fresh from the City?

Getting good information is only half of it. How we communicate is the next big hurdle. I know we've heard it so many times before, but getting good communication is critical for a well-run team. Everybody is valued, and playing their part in the team. The shepherd often uses a whistle to get his message across to the dogs but a lot can be gestures as well. Just knowing what the others are doing and how they will react makes life/work a lot easier.

If you can get that synergistic way of working, so that everybody knows instinctively what to do, life becomes so much easier. Once this has been achieved it becomes hard to change. This is so true with the sheep when they know which way to run from field to field - and in the handling system (how we organise the flow of the sheep) they know the routine making the shepherd's work easier. The old sheep teach the young lambs, and changing that for the sheep and the dogs can be difficult. The sheep and dogs all know the system and what is expected. Change has to be handled carefully. If the process flows well, not changing it is the easier thing to do, but of course it does not encourage thinking outside the box or field.

As a shepherd I often get asked to give advice about how to treat a sheep and I think this is interesting because there are so many pitfalls. Somebody will describe something and you'll create a picture in your own mind, and they will want you to diagnose the problem. The challenge is that they can forget some of the detail that can be so important. Describe something and you're only conveying such a small amount of the big picture. Often we assume that it's the environment, what's happened in the past, or the history of the animal. I find myself painting in colour which might not be right;

after all how many shades of green grass are there?

This could be called detail, but it is important to get the whole picture. You can give specifics but it is a lot harder to paint the whole picture in such detail without being there.

For me, I find it really difficult to be able to diagnose something over the phone. The quick call is just not enough information to create the real picture and even with the use of film it can still get distorted. We all have different reference points and we need to eliminate them first. For example how big is "big" and how heavy is "heavy"?

Everybody has a different size and weight in mind. Giving a figure does help but we still don't know if it is heavy or awkward.

When Foot and Mouth Disease broke out, the vets needed to describe every part of the sheep's mouth. To get some clarity, they described the mouth of the sheep in Latin terms and the language was very targeted. Nevertheless, their diagnosis was faulty because they were trying to describe it to a third party on the phone, so a lot of misdiagnosis happened. They were not actually present, and there were only a few people who had seen the disease first hand. It was felt that the few people should stay in London to give their best decision on whether or not the sheep had the disease. The challenge was that the vets had not looked in many healthy sheep mouths but so-called unqualified shepherds had. As a consequence the vets had to build up a large amount of knowledge very quickly and in retrospect make a better diagnosis. In fact, through Foot and Mouth the shepherds were best placed to make the diagnosis because they knew their sheep; they could say if the sheep were well or not.

Not making use of all the resources around you can promote strong feelings, resentment and even hatred. Knowing what was normal and what wasn't, through experience and being there at the time, was in fact more valuable than all the Latin names in the world. So understanding your team, what they have to offer in terms of experience and exploring all their thoughts will keep everybody on the same side.

Most people will talk in code at some time.

It is normally when they are asking you a tricky question, so they talk in "code". It is up to you to assess if they are asking the real question and not an easy question to see what the response will be. They really want you to listen more and ask them a question so they can explain more. How you react to all the questions is really important. Hurry on and dismiss it and you will never discover the real feeling, and that's where the trust is lost or gained.

The sheep will give only a small clue to indicate that it's not well. So we need to dig below the surface and understand what the real problem is and what we can do to help the animal. To get to any sort of success or any win-win situation, it is all about that understanding and trust. You don't necessarily have to agree with everybody's judgement, but you have to give validation, you have to allow them to have their say and give you time to observe everything.

Sheep. Shepherd. Dog.

Sometimes for sheep it can be a life or death situation, yet they outwardly don't show many signs, so observation is critically important. In the wild, showing weakness can be fatal for them, and actually that is the same with us; the more we show weakness, we more vulnerable we feel. Lowering our guard is hard for most people to do; it can show our vulnerable side, our Achilles heel. So what's the lesson here? Look and listen carefully.

http://bit.do/GoodShep

Chapter 4

A dog is a man's best friend - or is it?

Certainly in the shepherding world a dog is a faithful workmate. They come in many shapes and sizes, long-haired, short-haired, black, white and even tanned. For me, dogs perfectly illustrate the Olympics motto, "Citius, Altius, Fortius", which is Latin for "Faster, Higher, Stronger". Dogs are incredibly well-focused animals and yet they all have different styles and personalities.

You have the light-footed, Rough and Border Collies, which are like really good marathon runners: lean, fast, endurance, slick machines. Then there are the heavyweights, the sumo wrestler types, like the Old English Sheepdogs. They carry a lot more weight, are a lot more robust, yet still have a great ability to be able to stealthily move sheep. The big fluffy Dulux dog (as it is often known in the UK thanks to its long-term appearance in the paint brand adverts), goes bounding out in the field with all that hair going everywhere and using its voice, barking away at the sheep. They just love every minute, the more noise the better; they just want to work in a very energetic way, and have a very different style to other dogs.

By far the most popular of modern times in the UK is the Border Collie, the familiar black and white dog so often pictured with a shepherd. Widely known for its intelligence, it has a tremendously quick turn of speed and uses its eyes to move sheep. Its quickness to learn makes it a real delight to work with. It's subtle, it really has a presence about it and again love its work.

By contrast, the German Shepherd has good pace, it runs headlong going around the sheep, yet moves them by default. In reality it wants to protect them and to keep the sheep safe and separated from any predators, such as wolves, or other animals that would attack them. The dog has a protective nature and you can see how it's developed into more of a guard dog than a shepherd's dog.

The southern hemispheres have developed their own breeds: the New Zealand Huntaway and the Australian Kelpie, each of which have their own particular style and suitable strengths for herding sheep in the hot Antipodean climate.

Sheep. Shepherd. Dog.

Whatever the breed, I really think of the shepherd's dog as being in flow. They are just so passionate about getting a job done as well as they can, which make them phenomenal team members. They love what they do, they really want to work with you and they really are doing their thing - they're in the zone, in flow, whichever expression you want to use.

But the place we all start is where the dog wants to chase sheep. If any dog doesn't want to chase sheep you cannot teach it - the dog simply has to want to chase sheep. When you get a young puppy, you're so excited about getting it to see what its reaction is to sheep, but actually in a way you want to be able to hold it back. You want it to be at the right age so that it develops the correct way.

Often as shepherds we're quite excited to get a young puppy out into the field to see what it can do, but there is a great danger in this because it isn't fully grown. The legs of the puppy are not fully grown and the stamina of the puppy will quickly fade, and it will soon give up chasing the sheep. This can lead to the dog only ever chasing the backsides of the sheep, never being able to get in front of them, which means that it will always push sheep away from the shepherd. It won't ever learn that it can run around the front of the flock and face the sheep head on. Once this behaviour is learnt it can be potentially really damaging for the dog, as it takes a long time to work through and inspire its confidence.

Imagine if you're a young graduate and in your first week of work you're asked to give a big presentation to a key customer. You're keen to get on, wanting to impress, so you pull at your lead and bite at the task. When the day comes the key messages are missed and you fluff your lines. The whole thing leaves you feeling demoralised. Think how much encouragement it would take on the boss' part to inspire you to step up to the mark again.

So when introducing a puppy we must make sure that it knows who is master, who is boss, and puppy walking without any sheep around is such an important stage. Getting the basics right is crucial. I often think this is like when we go for a new job – we want to get the basics right from the very beginning. When building a team around you, how you want to start is how you're going to finish. Trying to knock bad habits out of dogs is so difficult. They're intelligent, they really want to work, and making sure you're on the right footing from the outset is imperative. If the dogs were left in the wild they would simply gang together and be unruly, as they'd want to work together. They would have a pecking order and they'd jockey for that top position and would work as a whole pack to kill and eat their feed.

When we're building a team, getting that "pack" feeling is really important. Getting that camaraderie and sense of togetherness overlaid with a sense of achievement builds the team identity.

It is not all about one person doing all the work; we know there is no "I" or "ewe" in team work.

It is all about what we want to achieve, and also making sure that the message of what we want out there, our purpose andour mission, is understood by everybody around us so that we can achieve it.

When the dogs have finished their work they look forward to going back and having time off, time in the kennels. Many people have said to me "Oh isn't it cruel, you ask them to work all day and then you put them in a kennel?" Well the good news is that the kennel is their place of safety where they can have time off as well as you. It allows the dogs some time to relax, think about what's happened during the day, inwardly digest, so that they can be more prepared for the next morning. I always think it's like us not having any time apart. Imagine living with your work colleagues 24 hours a day, working, playing, doing everything with your colleagues! It's great with a partner, but not necessarily with work colleagues; you would get rather tired and things might start to fray. There would be some adjustments to make.

So having time off to chill out and think about where you want to lead your team is really important for yourself as well as for the people/dogs. I think that's very true in business, and I know my business has grown every time I have come back from a decent break. Having holidays is so important; breaks, time to think and re-charge our batteries. It helps us to see things from a different angle.

In my working life I've only ever once worn out a Collie. We were working hard right up until one o'clock in the morning, moving sheep to get them to the next place. It's amazing with a full moon you can see so much, the dogs adapt to it and the sheep are quite happy to keep on going. It's often the coolest time of the day and often we find that actually starting early in the morning is the best time to wake everything up. On this occasion we had to load a lorry at five o'clock the following morning. This was the only time I've gone to the kennel when the dogs were so fast asleep that I had to ask them twice "Come on then, get up". They were looking at me through one eye as if to say "What do you mean, get up so soon?"!

The great thing is that they very quickly turn that attitude around. They are so focused on their work, it's as if they're thinking "Oh alright, okay we're off again" and they immediately get in the Land Rover, ready to go to work. That to me is a great attitude. If you've got people like that around you, think what you can do.

There was one other time that the dogs didn't quite do as they were told. I'd left the dogs behind with my partner so she could get the sheep in when I was returning later in the day. The dogs had done it hundreds of times before and I thought it would be OK because she used to feed them occasionally; they knew the place, they knew the field, and it was at home, so surely they would work. I phoned her up and asked her to get the sheep in. I immediately thought that when the telephone call came back it would be good news, that the sheep had all gone in, they're ready for us, but alas she said, no, the dogs won't move. I immediately accused her of not doing something right, but it was nothing to do with that. She'd stood in the right place, had given the right commands and the dogs just simply looked at her. So I asked for her to put the phone to the dog's ear. I said those magic words, "away to me", and off the dog shot like a rocket, round the sheep. But halfway round she pulled up a bit short as if to ask "but where are you?" It just shows you that one dog and one man do need to work together.

How valuable would that be in business, to have a loyal workforce that doesn't compromise your integrity or your values? That must be worth a fortune. On the flip-side if your team will act only upon your command, possibly because they don't feel empowered to do otherwise, you could become indispensable.

http://bit.do/No1Dog

Chapter 5

K.I.S.S. – Keep It Simple, Shepherd (for the sheep)

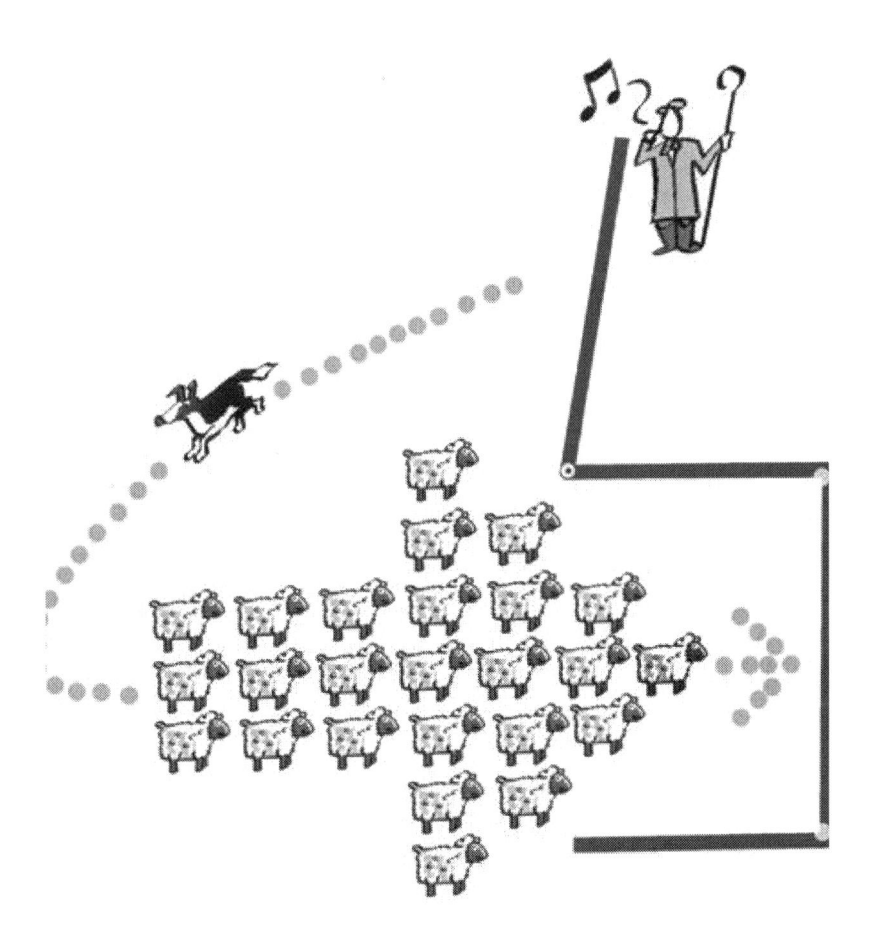

The relationship between the sheep and the shepherd is really important. What is really necessary is a clear plan of what you as the shepherd want to achieve. As a consequence we have a process and nothing's more clear than this process at lambing time. A good system is easy to follow, contains a lot of relevant information and is so simple that everybody can follow it, regardless of whether you've been working with sheep before. The real test is whether somebody just walking in can work the system. You might have just five minutes' chat with them and they will understand what you need from them. For me it is about the transfer of knowledge and knowing what is important to do in which order. Being able to move on to the next task, with confidence, knowing you are in control and following a system.

Time is precious at lambing time. There's a limit to what time can be spent with just one sheep, otherwise the other sheep will be neglected. Just like hospitals, the longer the sheep and their young lambs stay indoors the more chances they have of picking up some disease. This is the incentive for the system to work efficiently as this drives down costs. Antibiotics can be a backup plan but this can slow the whole process down. To keep the system simple and effective, a review is held every year. Data from the sheep is gathered, scrutinised and any improvements made. Reviewing is a key part to every business, even in the sheep world.

The better the information gathered, the more productive you will get. For example, at lambing time some of the ewes get a bit confused about which lambs are their's. So the shepherd marks the lambs that belong to the ewe by spraying corresponding numbers or letters on the side of the ewe and its lamb. The ewe generally uses her sense of smell to identify her lambs but as we can't do this, the marking is our way of identification. You can pair up the right animals to the right sheep, which works incredibly well. You can just start with the number one and go upwards.

The question I asked myself was:

is there any more information we can glean without using any more paint on the small lamb?

Put this another way, is there an alternative way of approaching a traditional system, thinking outside the box, always asking why are we doing this and whether we can we find a simpler system or process. With the sheep it is easy to forget which number you have reached, especially when dealing with a large flock, and if just using numbers you can run out of space once you get into the hundreds on a small newborn lamb. So is there a better code we can use?

For myself, I always dot the single lambs that correspond with the ewe. With single sheep they are less likely to lose one, so as long as you see a sheep with a dotted lamb it's 99% likely to be correct. I number the twins and use different colours to avoid long numbers. For multiple births I use letters of the alphabet. That way when I'm looking at the lambs out in the field I know instantly what I'm looking at, single, twin or more. Knowing it's a twin instantly means that I don't have to remember loads of numbers. I would also know that a ewe with just one lamb at her side with a number on the side must have another one around. I know it's a triplet as there is A, B, C on the lamb's side.

When faced with a lot of information, it needs to be easy to understand and useful for all parties using it. In my experience some systems do work but rely a lot on technology, rather than a simple system. The simpler (often the less technological!) the system is, the less it can go wrong. Take simple traffic lights; everybody knows what each colour means and knows how to react. Once you've understood any system you instantly get to work in the field in my case.

Should you use spray markers or ear tags? The painting system can be accurate with the identification of individual sheep/lambs by their numbers, but is not permanent, only lasting two to three months at best. Ear tags, on the other hand, last a lifetime, as long as they stay put, but can be easily misread, and double-checking is very wasteful on valuable time. Misreading happens for lots of reasons, such as sheep moving around, not staying put in a pen or simple human error, all of which make clear identification hard to achieve. Having a clear goal of what you want to achieve and why, and keeping things as simple as possible makes us more productive.

Let me explain why tags don't work well at lambing time. We first need to catch the lambs and the ewe, read the ear tag by machine or eye, make a note of the numbers and look them up to see if they are meant to be together, whereas the spray marking is simply a look at the sheep and match-up of the marks. Ear tags are expensive on time, not friendly to use in this case, and very reliant on technology. The plus side is that the eartags are more prominent and can help with long-term information compared to the paint system.

We can place the ear tags in either ear but I choose to specify the location of the ear tag, as this can add information itself. Placed in the left ear can mean, it's "left in for another chance", so it might stay in the flock for another season if it does not put another foot wrong. This is a bit like a yellow card in a football match. If it's in the right ear, like the red card in the football match, it's "right out with no second chance". For me this is simple to remember (left in, right out), there's no need to remember any numbers and it's also very distinctive. Any sheep with a right ear tag I know will not go to the ram next time. Just by simply looking at the ewe it helps me to remember it as an individual rather than part of a mass.

Remembering the detail is hard but it is made easier with crib notes. Sometimes it is easier to note what you are not looking for as this might be less than what you are looking for. Turning things upside down can work as long as everybody understands the big picture of what you want to achieve.

Building a system that works for your team and committing to it will get the results.

The skill of shepherding has a lot to do with detail. Treating the whole animal and not jumping in with the first idea is really important. We need to gain all the information about how the sheep have reacted to this point. It's a bit like when people ask a question, almost like a tester, to see how that goes, and only if that goes well will they ask the next real question. Hurry on, don't give time to answer the first question and you might not find out the next question which is really the question they wanted answering in the first place. Just as we shepherds look at the whole animal and treat every bit of it. The slight hint of weakness will give us a big clue as to how to treat the sheep. In the wild, that hint of weakness would be picked up by their predators and would be singled out and attacked. So the sheep would not want to show any weakness, otherwise they would be picked on, and if they were not feeling so well the predators would home in on them.

Humans can act the same way.

The ability to be vulnerable can be seen as a weakness

and yet it can help us develop people. Having a clearer understanding of where they're coming from and being able to develop their skills, just like we do with a young dog.

This leads onto

being able to see things from a different point of view.

We have to remember that most of us view our world from about five to six foot up in the air, but the sheep and the dog are so much lower, just over a couple of feet at best. When it appears that we can see a clear way through a gateway or into a pen, the animals can't see the bigger picture. They see it from two feet high, and often seeing it at that level makes a huge difference. Affixing a camera to the sheep and dog has been a real eye-opener to me in recent years! Even though I have worked with the sheep for many years, having a camera on the sheep's head so you can see what they are looking at, has made me realise how quickly sheep make up their minds. They see an opportunity and go for it. No half-heartedness about them as long as their head is looking in that direction they are off and invariably running.

Sheep won't go through what appears to be a solid wall. It's similar to when we walk into a public toilet,; we generally need to go right into a corner before we can see the exit. If we can't actually judge that the two walls don't line up, they appear to be connected as one solid wall. This would be very difficult for a sheep to judge, as they don't have great binocular vision, unless they were right in the corner. The sheep don't naturally don't like to be trapped. But if one of the flock disappears around the corner it is intrigued to know where that sheep's gone and ventures after it.

http://bit.do/KISS

The Sheep are running round and round a car and as soon as one goes round the corner, the rest follow. Going round the next corner more sheep follow until it ends up with a mob running round and round this car. The thought that the sheep in front is getting away to "freedom" makes the rest follow. From their perspective they only see it from two feet up, but because we see it from six feet up it looks completely different. The sheep run round and round the car, and even though the car is still moving forward, they just simply run faster and faster!

The fear of missing out is so great it can drive us to do extraordinary things. Just think how people act when wanting a bargain in January or on Black Friday. This can lead to a level of frustration that can cause unhelpful reactions. The human fear of loss is often manipulated by salespeople as a tactic: "this offer is available today only" or even the over-used phrase "buy now to avoid disappointment".

By contrast the fear of not achieving can be used as an encouragement, motivating people to go further, faster, longer. It can keep the energy high in the team and can be done by giving genuine praise. Conveying positive and encouraging messages to your team is far more effective than limiting it to the more traditional annual appraisal.

Sheep are creatures of habit and once they have done something a few times they will get very used to it, just like people and their routine of going to work. When you suddenly take it away there is a void so they fill the time with something else, yet will still remember the old days and will soon go back if they enjoyed it. This is the same with the sheep; once they've gotten used to being fed or moving from one field to the next, they will tend to run back to where they already know. So if we move them from one field to the next they will tend to run back to the previous field. Over a time they get to know all the fields on the farm where they can get food. Why? - because they understand the routine and are just looking for an easy life.

As a shepherd you really get to know your sheep; what they can achieve, how they'll react. Every flock is different. Working with people we get to know them, if they are not in a good mood or if they are away from anything "normal". It makes our interaction with them easier.

Every shepherd works with his sheep slightly differently and as a consequence when we take over we need to be able to adapt to other people's sheep. What we often find is that the sheep are used to a certain way of working under the guidance of that shepherd. Consequently it's better to stick with the routine as much as possible, only changing elements one by one. Doing it one step at a time is less arduous than introducing a whole new process at once.

Sometimes we can find out a great reason why the shepherd worked the way he did and we might adapt our plan. If a plan doesn't work really well, we need to adapt quickly to make the most of the situation. Let's say we're trying to get the sheep in the pen, and we find it's not big enough, no-one else is about; what can we do without letting the sheep all go out into the field again? The sheep are in stand-off mode, refusing to co-operate. Time to be flexible and adapt our original plan. We might adjust the pen, make it bigger, open it up and make a bigger space. These are all things that make the pen more attractive for the sheep to go into. That's the flexibility and ability to "move on", look forward and not get bogged down with ego or blame.

Chapter 6

Assessing the right dog for the team

How do you pick a good dog for yourself? Firstly you have to remember that at least 50% of the team is your dog, and not every dog will work for you, nor will you like every dog you see. I guess like most occupations there's a job interview, some more formal than others but nevertheless it is a way of getting to know each other and to see if the necessary working skills and attitude are present.

Much of it comes down to gut feeling and instinct, influenced by our experience. With a young puppy we can simply see which one comes out of the litter to us, and we feel some sort of a connection. The great news is that it is a blank canvas and we can create our dog, the way we want it, within the limits of its ability. It will get to know our mannerisms; it will get to know us and the way we work, as well as the routine we like to have. On the other hand, when selecting an older dog it is really necessary to have that long "interview" process, drilling down and finding out whether they fit in with us or not. Invariably we get a few weeks' trial, a probationary period similar to new staff at work. During this time we need to assess their character and behaviour traits; by pushing them to see how much they can do or not. As with people, it takes a little time for dogs to settle in, and their first reactions can be different to the long-term results. It is a judgement call on whether they will fit in with the team or not, just like any employment scenario.

When the chips are down we really rely on the dog to pull something out of the bag, to avoid a situation from deteriorating further. Such as when the sheep are running at high speed in the wrong direction, heading towards a main road, how are we and our dog going to react? This can be made worse when the dog rounds up 99% of the sheep but leaves one or two still going towards the main road. Do they react better to the verbal command? If we start to raise our voice do they panic or freeze on the spot? Or do they respond better with a whistle, giving clear, precise directions with little tonality? Keeping calm and simply giving them our intention, our plan, will they react well to us? This is when 100% confidence is needed in the dog every time. When we're both working in that adventure zone, doing something we haven't done before can be difficult and it all comes down to how we communicate and respond to each other.

Sheep. Shepherd. Dog.

A good team will know how each member will react,

what information they need and how they need to receive it. Knowing each person's strengths (and weaknesses) is critical to prompting the best behaviour and will help get the task done.

I always think of the rubber band and the rock. If you try and move a rock with a rubber band there are three possible outcomes. The first is the rubber band will overstretch and break, the rock doesn't move and the task was too great for the band. The second possibility is you keep pulling at the rubber band and eventually the rock will move, at high speed at first, yet it might hit the front of the band as it moves. The third possibility is by applying the right amount of variable force the rock moves forward at an even pace, the rubber band doesn't break through being overstretched and the rock moves to where you need it.

In this ever-faster world of instant gratification we all look to get things done quickly, so cutting corners is often seen as the solution. Achieving more out of less is attractive provided the principles stay the same.

If the dog starts to cut corners on its out-run it starts to head straight towards the sheep. Instead of the sheep gently moving towards the shepherd, they will run at best to one side or at worst away from the shepherd. This may sound a small point as the dog will quickly get round the front of the sheep, but over time keeping a nice pear shape in the out-run gives the best result with calmer sheep, as they have taken the direct route towards the shepherd.

Establishing our values at the outset and keeping to them will allow the dogs to work well with us. Short-cutting a system may work for a while but eventually fails because the third party (sheep, customer, colleague) moves in any direction rather than becoming loyal and attracted to you.

One thing the dog really does need is consistency in the shepherd's (its master's) behaviour. Our instructions must be clear about what we need it to do, whilst empowering it to do the right thing. Often with a clear and simple end goal, what are we trying to achieve is all that is given. For the dog this is too big a picture they need one step at a time. When we give the command to stop or lie down, what is really meant is to stop in the right place, remaining connected to and in control of the sheep. Often it looks like the dog just drops as soon as it hears the command but that is just the shepherd and the dog working well together. The reward in the dog's mind is being fed at the end of the day, being looked after, being part of the gang that gets things done. Just like people you can wind a dog up: you ask it to do the same thing four or five times and it gets wound up and starts to bite the sheep, obviously not what we want. This applies to both parties if the shepherd doesn't perform the dog also gets wound up with him!

I remember once holding the sheep with the dog in the corner of a field, for a novice shepherd to catch just any one sheep. After five attempts of not catching a single one, he as well as the dogs understandably got frustrated. The dogs felt they were doing their part, but why was the shepherd not doing his? The goal was not too big for the novice, but there was a distinct lack of focus. Every time he went in to catch a sheep, they moved away from him. It appeared to the novice shepherd that other sheep where closer and so he kept changing his mind.

Working as a team is very much a two-way process. We have to perform as well as our team members for everything to come together. Setting clear, focused and achievable goals after an incident like I've described here is really important in order to regain the confidence and trust of the team. Helping them stay focused on one sheep no matter what happens around them was a key point in their life.

Nevertheless everybody needs to be stretched, and making mistakes is how we grow, but how do we apologise? Do we even need to apologise? And if so, how do we do it? Do we apologise to the dogs? I do when I make an error, as I feel it is only right to correct the matter straight away. It has been known for me to confuse left with right and I find that the dog is going the right way but not the way I've commanded! In other words, left has now become right and has right has now become left. We must have a truce where I stop the dog and confess "okay the silly shepherd got it wrong". Does it mean I'm a poor shepherd? No, I don't believe it does. It simply means I've recognised that I didn't get something quite right; the dog accepts that and starts again. The important thing is that the dog was empowered to do the right thing even though the command was not necessarily correct. Wouldn't it be great to have a team that do the right thing, even though you gave the wrong command? An apology can be appropriate at times; it shows we're only human and it conveys an element of humility to the team around you. Ultimately this will grow respect.

Building your team by empowering the people around you to do the right thing makes a very strong and robust team. So it would be a great command to say to the dog, just get all the sheep in this pen. But unfortunately that would be a too big a command for the dog to take on. It needs a bit more detail and at the right pace in order to achieve this. Breaking the information down into bite sizes such as "go round the back of the sheep", "stop (in the right place)" and "move left/move right a bit". Giving the dog confidence and actually allowing it to do it in a way that is comfortable is key to keeping control of the sheep. It is your job as a shepherd to be able to set up the situation knowing that the sheep you want will end up in a pen, making sure you've got enough room, while making life easy for getting them in the pen in the first place. In a competition, i.e. a sheepdog trial, when you are required to do the difficult task of herding just a few sheep in the pen, you have to be in perfect synchronicity with your dog. It isn't about the commands you're saying, it is the way you give encouragement to the dog so that it can work at its full potential. The commands are about reassurance and direction, which helps it to do the right thing. Working together to get the sheep in the pen with all those nerves jangling in a competitive situation is such a hard task.

We all get tested throughout our lives. In our early years it is how we are judged but as we get older we can choose not to be challenged. I always refer to this saying, which could well have come from a farmer:

You are either green and growing or are ripe and rotten.

It's your choice which stage you want to be in!

http://bit.do/RDog

Chapter 7

How would ewe react to the dog?

How does the sheep really view the dog? The sheep's instinct is to move away from the dog. It's a real threat to the sheep. The dog moves faster than the sheep, it has teeth and can bite, it can outpace the sheep and if it was an out of control dog it would ultimately kill and eat the sheep. So it is a wise precaution for the sheep to move away at some pace. The safest place for the sheep is in the middle of the flock, where all the others are protecting it, and it's only the ones on the outside that would be attacked. In the wild the weaker ones would be pushed to the outside and therefore would almost be that sacrificial lamb.

Ultimately the sheep are scared; they have feelings of anxiety, and after a dog attack they are very uptight in the field. For us it's the equivalent of something hanging over us like paying the taxman, or waiting for some life or death results; it is not the most comfortable experience. We have feelings of dread and loathing. Or is it the feeling that the taxman won't spend our money as wisely as we would?!

Walking into a roomful of strangers where you feel that all eyes will be looking at us would cause most of us to feel a level of anxiety. This would be very similar to a sheep running away from the protection and safety of the flock, even though there are times when it chooses to separate itself from the flock. It's amazing what decisions both sheep and people will make in this situation. Once isolated from the flock the sheep might well, especially if the dog is close behind, go into a "blind panic" where they will run and run as far as they can in one direction, not turning left or right, but simply keep going. Whatever obstacle is in the way they will try and jump, get through or barrel into it at high speed, hoping that it will break.

Blind panic can often be seen on TV 'reality' shows where people are put under stress

and they make the most ridiculous conclusions and theories, causing them to react in abnormal ways. Later on when they've had time to reflect they realise that they have done silly things, not really understanding why they made those irrational comments or actions. I guess that is the importance of friends, family and close colleagues that you can rely on. When the sheep are in that blind panic it is easier to bring the flock to the isolated one and surround it with the calming effect of the flock. This way you can bring it back into the fold and it will start to calm down very quickly.

Can the sheep dominate the dog? Can it defeat the threat of the dog? Of course this can happen quite easily at lambing time when the incentive for the ewe with its little lamb at foot is to protect it, and will override any natural fear of running away. The ewe would beat the dog with its head, which is very hard, and will pummel it if the dog is trapped, and will absolutely deter the dog from ever, ever looking at another sheep again. This will have lasting damage on the dog and it will never challenge a sheep head on, it will always dart away and back off. Not great for a shepherd wanting to work with that dog: every time you want the dog to push the sheep into the pen it will never have the confidence or the authority to do so.

When people are really riled and they feel very emotional about a subject, they will go to the ends of the earth to prove their point. This will lead them often to make irrational decisions, sometimes even employing lawyers, at vast expense, to help them argue their case. They believe they're on the moral high ground and will blindly pursue their point without any rational thought.

When there are two or more dogs working, the sheep are actually not doubly stressed, they actually accept the inevitable a lot more quickly. They will be in a tighter bunch and you can move them more easily because they are more accepting of where the dogs are, and they know they just have to go in one direction.

Similarly, when there is a perception of overwhelming force on a group it will be more compliant to obeying the word of authority. For example, at a football match there are more supporters than police and if it came to a one-to-one battle the police would clearly be outnumbered. However, as they are well organised and have authority they can control the crowds. You will always get one or two rebels but the group can calm these people down if given the chance.

So what is the dog's feeling towards the sheep? Well, it's just doing its job. It wants to do the best it possibly can. It wants to do it quickly and efficiently, and it's quite happy to throw its weight around. It backs up its intentions with action. There are no second thoughts. It's as if it is saying "If you're coming towards me sheep, I'm in control here; I'm going to turn you round." The dog has that cocky ability to know what he does, and he does it well. He can master these animals, even if he gets a slight little duffing over by a sheep who gets one over on him, he will be back quicker than quick. He will be back on his feet as if to say "you're not doing that again."

As with all things there are exceptions to the rule, and often this comes around when working with pet sheep. The sheep get very used to the dog coming in to the field, not hassling them; they get very used to the dog just wandering around doing its own thing. I've even seen sheep cuddle up to dogs when they are cold, even though the natural thing for the sheep is to run away. The dog could take advantage of this situation and easily overpower the sheep, but because of the circumstances, i.e. they are both pets, both animals feel comfortable with this. When another dog, which isn't a pet, comes in to the field the sheep are slightly wary but they play the same game as if it is the pet dog, and they suddenly find it has a different attitude. The ears will go up as if to say: "Oh my gosh, I've just been nipped on the back end, I'd better run away" and soon it's back to the natural way of the sheep always running away from the dog.

When a new leader is appointed the team usually continues with the same behaviour, which doesn't necessarily work with the new management style. Authority is asserted and the team adjust their behaviours they are forced to change. This is when respect for the new manager is either gained or lost. Just like the dog, the management needs to be backed up so the natural order is regained.

http://bit.do/EweDog

Chapter 8

Building that magnificent team

Is team building really needed or is it just a jolly and an excuse for time off work? Does it have any lasting effect on the way people work together, and will it have a positive impact on the bottom line?

Often when working with a team you've simply been introduced, told to get on with it and get great results. There might have been changes at many levels and for a myriad of reasons: people have been added to or let go, roles re-defined, targets altered, and so on. There are all sorts of reasons why these changes happen, such as reshuffles, redeployments, down-sizing, just to name a few. All of these things can contribute to teams not working well together in the beginning.

Uncertainty of how colleagues will react to the situation in which the team finds itself is possibly why most people will not speak up. They might fear losing their job, standing out from the others or ending up being marked as a troublemaker in the group. Let's face it, few things stay static for long, and the team dynamic is either strengthening or falling apart. Nevertheless, working together to achieve a common goal can achieve so much more, and more efficiently, than a random bunch of individuals.

It is not often you get a blank piece of paper on which to construct a well-balanced team. More often the team is built with the people we inherit and we are expected to magically gel this team together to meet high expectation targets without leaving the coalface. Is this really the best way of creating a well-oiled machine? Is just the practice of "doing" enough to achieve outstanding results or is it better to inspire the people to become the best they can be? Even if there's a bus strike, for example, making it hard to get to work, they will still go the extra mile for the team's sake, otherwise they feel they will be letting the rest of the team down. In reality, most teams cannot afford to carry passengers.

Most leaders are judged on how quickly they get the results, and not the journey the team has gone through.

Often people need time to grow, and that happens best when trust and a no-blame culture is encouraged.

So what questions would really help to pull your team together? And in what context would it be best to ask them? A change of routine and environment is a great start, before even thinking about the questions, and often this will take the form of an external team building away day.

What are the components of an awesome team building event and what form should it take?

Just taking the team out for a drink can be a great way for pulling people together, although not everybody drinks alcohol of course. Having time to celebrate what has been achieved so far provides a fabulous opportunity to understand the way your colleagues like to work best. Communication within the team, how they like to receive and give out information, can be talked about during this time. The down-side can be that it can go too far and degenerate into ….. - or is that just young farmers?!

In the sheep world it is similar to two different flocks being put in the same field. The sheep will keep in their different groups, slightly separated with their individual circle of influence around them, only briefly communicating with the other group. After a long time they will become one, but although when under stress they will often run back to their original flocks.

When you share a meal as a team, there can be more interaction as it concentrates people on talking to one another for a longer time. There is something about eating and sharing of food that really helps bond people together. It's a ritual that has taken place since biblical times.

I am not sure why, but it is the same in the animal world. If we mix two different flocks together they will remain in their original flocks until we feed them. Where there is limited good food, the sheep have to jostle against each other to get their fair share. After a week or so the flock starts to work as a cohesive unit, once they have worked out their differences and they will really bond together, just as we do in our teams.

There are will always be people who don't shine in some situations; the louder, more confident people will undermine the shy, retiring types who can often be overlooked. Just as within a flock of sheep there will always be one bold, adventurous bully grabbing more than its fair share of the food. We need to look out for this, otherwise both sets of sheep (the ones getting too much or not enough food) will have problems.

Even though time in the pub or having a meal can be useful bonding time for a team and it will has its place, how can you stretch the team to find out what they are really capable of? I feel this can only really be done when pushing the team into what I call the adventure zone, where everybody is slightly uncomfortable. This is not about making them do things that in later life they might regret, but asking them to get away from the norm of work, trying something they have not done before which that will promote "new" thinking. An activity that could start new habits, engender the trust of others as they are really having to work together to achieve better results. Interrupting old habits and asking the team to think in a new way is so powerful. Pattern interrupters can be hard to achieve, but the rewards will almost always be worth the effort.

So what are the qualities of an outstanding team building event? Firstly it should have a clear purpose of what you want to achieve. If it's just a good time, a laugh, that's fine, and having a drink or BBQ will do that. If more is wanted, a deeper understanding of the team and how they tick, then the following points will really help:

#1 The task should be challenging as well as having a strong element of fun. We tend to learn more when laughing and enjoying ourselves. There should be no room for passengers: everybody must have a vital role to play in achieving the task.

#2 The rules should be simple to follow, not too many of them as this will allow some experimentation and creativity to develop within the team. This encourages out of the box thinking and creativity to be valued.

#3 A level of unpredictability in the task: the more uncertainty the task offers, the more it will challenge the group, and working together will be promoted.

#4 An activity as far removed from their normal working environment as possible. This allows a break in the normal roles people play in the team, and the chance to explore new ones.

#5 The requirement for excellent communication so that everybody has to chip in their ideas and communicate at a level which is appropriate for the task. The need for encouragement across the team has a key role to play.

#6 Trusting other team members, being able to empower each one as an individual to fulfill a vital part in completing the task.

#7 A level of difficulty where there is a chance the task may not be achieved. This leads to a greater experience of success gives after a period of doubt and most likely frustration.

#8 An increasing level of difficulty whereby incentives can be used to encourage completion as well as introduce an element of competition if desired.

#9 The activity offers a level playing field for all the team. No one individual has a solution which that can direct the group to success.

#10 A task which that encourages the team to look at each situation from a different perspective. Analogies with your business can be drawn from the way in which the task is approached.

Ultimately, what lessons from the team building activity can be taken back to the workplace? Can you be sure that all ideas on the day were listened to and explored further at a subsequent review session? This makes the exercise very relevant to how the team works, and how it is going to move forward in the future. This can be done in a variety of different ways but is often overlooked. Making time for this feedback three or four weeks after the team build really helps to ensure that the learning points have been grasped, adopted by and, importantly, owned by the group.

Feedback workshops cover so many aspects, including:
- communication – the feelings that were involved and what worked best to get the most out of the team
- trust – the trust of the group consensus is far more powerful than any one individual, allowing everyone to develop a sense of camaraderie
- creativity – how it helped to use creativity to explore the endless possibilities and the fun that was had in so doing
- incentives – how were they best used, which ones really worked and why
- decision-making – which ways helped the team to achieve success
- leadership – how the shepherd inspired his team of 'dogs' to great effect

The analogies and metaphors are endless when transferring the lessons into the normal working environment, as you might imagine.

So how many of the criteria listed above can you tick off for your next team building programme? If it's less than

Sheep. Shepherd. Dog.

10, get in touch with us at Raising the Baa – and why not benefit from my special offer (overleaf) to you as a reader of this book…

http://bit.do/Magteam

An exclusive offer from the author (aka Head Shepherd) to readers of this book

Dear reader

Firstly thank you for taking the time to read this, my first book. I still find it hard to believe that I've actually written a book. My English teacher at school would be even more surprised, I would imagine! The 3 R's were not my strength at school, certainly not helped by undiagnosed (at the time) dyslexia; however, since I was set on going into farming from childhood I wasn't the most diligent of students in these areas. So to see my name as an author is still quite surreal!

I have shared many of the stories contained within these pages as a public speaker and it's thanks to the various audiences who suggested I write a book. Most of these people have been entrepreneurs or in the corporate world so when networking afterwards many have asked questions about Raising the Baa and how we attract major corporate names.

If you've found the narrative to be engaging and interesting, then I **know** that you and your team will discover so much more during (and after) our team building with sheep programmes.

So I'm offering you an exclusive gift

**Two FREE places
at our Open Ewe-niversity
- test-drive
a Raising the Baa
team building programme***

Take a look at this video to get a flavour of what to expect on a Raising the Baa programme and hear what some of our clients have to say too: http://bit.do/BaaPreview

Sheep. Shepherd. Dog.

And if you like what you see, get in touch with one of the flock.

Wishing you the best in building the most awesome team in your field.

Chris

* Offer is subject to availability and may change without notice.

About the Author – Chris Farnsworth

Born and bred in London, Chris' early ambition was to be a farmer but perhaps this was an idyllic childhood dream? Despite the hard work, the adverse British weather and the likelihood of low remuneration, he pursued his passion and made a few opportunities to work in the countryside on farms. This experience earned him a place at Hampshire's agricultural college, Sparsholt.

Chris did not discover his talent with sheep until he travelled to Australia and New Zealand where he sampled the lifestyle of a shepherd. He returned to the UK and started a life as a contract shepherd, managing other people's flocks as well as having his own sheep. At the peak of his shepherding career, when Chris looked after 6500 sheep with the aid of just two dogs, however, his business took a nose-dive as a result of Foot and Mouth disease.

Without any other job skills, Chris turned his hand to direct selling! Initially promoting aloe vera products to help animals and their owners with their health, Chris built up an international team of Forever distributors through perseverance, mentoring and coaching. As a regional trainer for the company, Chris often used analogies from the shepherding world, illustrating the synergy with business, in particular how individuals interact.

With a desire to give back to the community, a chance meeting with the founder of a youth charity led to the creation of 'team building with sheep'. The experience challenges a team of people to herd sheep, doing the job of both shepherd and dog. Commercial organisations soon became interested and Raising the Baa was launched in 2011.

Away from sheep, Chris enjoys travel, hiking, photography, a glass of good red wine or his local 6X beer and creating really useful stuff from recycled materials (you should see the garage!).

Chris lives with his partner in rural Wiltshire with a dog, a cat and several flocks of sheep.

@sheepshepherddog
@raisingthebaa

@raisingthebaa

www.facebook.com/raisingthebaa

ShepherdChrisFarnsworth

www.raisingthebaa.com

Made in the USA
Charleston, SC
19 November 2015